I0556961

Thanks to all those who inspired this book.

Thanks to all those who will inspire more.

Obssessions

copyright 1998
chris haley

OBSESSIONS
Copyright © 1998 by Chris Haley
All rights reserved. This book or any portion thereof may not be reproduced or used in any manner whatsoever without the express written permission of the author except for the use of brief quotations in a book review.
Printed in the United States of America
First Printing, 1998
Second Printing, 2021
ISBN# 978-0-9993579-2-7

OBSESSIONS

chris haley

1998

Photographs by Dave Millspaugh

Edited by Ricardo Lizardi

how things change...

How things change
And remain the same
A different occupation
A different home;
The same obsessions
The same unknowns.

The psychic would have
Destroyed me
Who would have predicted
These hard times to come
But escape is never an option from
The course life must run.

I have faith,
I have hope,
I believe one day
When my search is fulfilled
I'll laugh at the frustrations that
Haunted me
And revel in the
Resolve of my will.

Different faces, changed places,
Foreign streets to roam.
How funny I fled my
Last heartache
To find the same obsessions
The same unknowns.

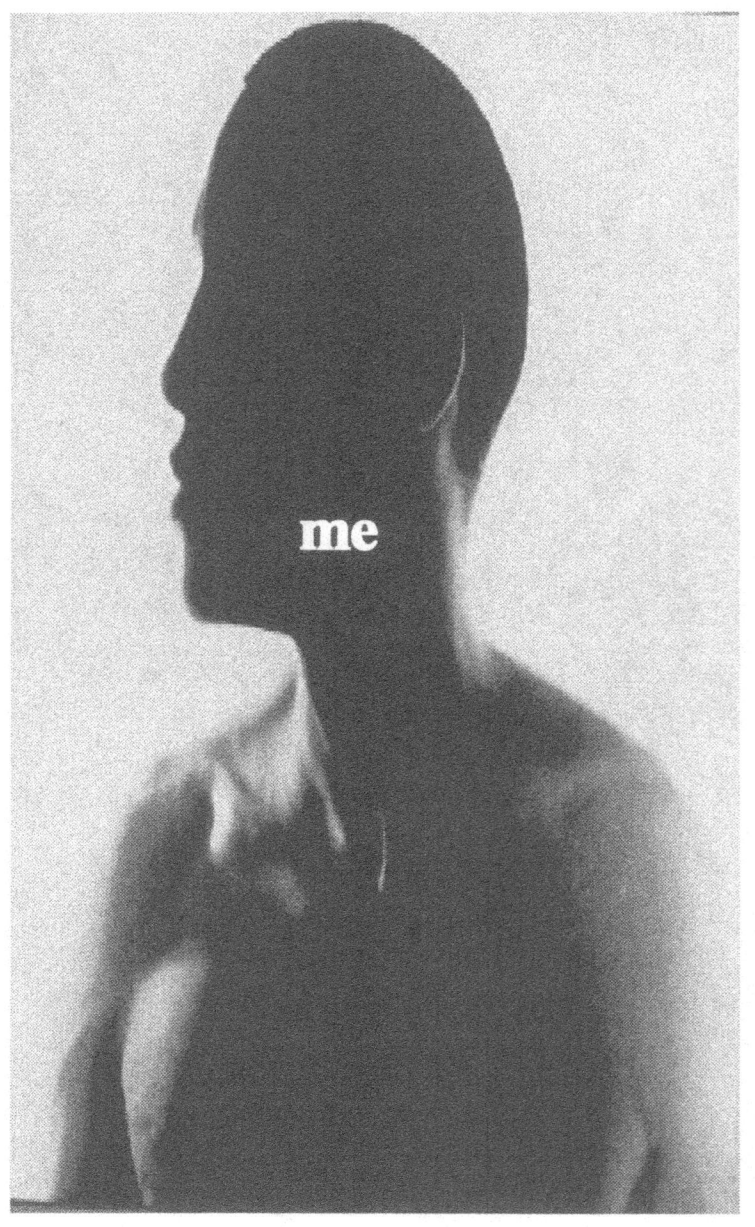

me

The biggest obsession

How do I look?
Are you looking at me?
Why are you looking?
Do you like what you see?

Do you like my appearance
Do I make you hot
Do you want to see more
Do you like what I got

Are you watching me walk
Are you drawn to my style
Are you wishing you had me
Are you craving a smile?

What do you think of my clothes
Do they fit me just right
Loose where it doesn't matter
And where it does, sooo tight.

Why don't you approach me
What are you waiting for
Do I remind you of someone you'd forgotten
Do you think if we spoke
You'd be bored

I can't stand here forever
They're others who want me, too.
Make your move now or forget it
I'm going to count to...102.

All right
That's it
I'm leaving!
I've got better things to do
Unless you stop me when I walk by
That's your last chance
If not, we're through.

Okaaaay
I'm at the door
You're playing too hard to get
I'll look at you one more time
Then I'm out of here
You're not making me sweat.

Look
Don't take for granted
I'll show up again
Its a weekday night
I'm usually in
You're lucky I appeared this time...
All right then
I'm walking
I'm out the door...
Fine.

What was it
Why didn't you talk to me
What did you want
What didn't you see?

I was right there
We were eye to eye
I'm not ugly
I'm goodlooking
I know I am
Why didn't you try

I hate this
Why was I shy
What's wrong with me
I wanna die
Why couldn't I be
More confident, more assured
Why didn't I say something
Will I ever be cured
Why do I always have to be...
me.

ROOTS
This part of me

Whenever I watch ROOTS
Whenever I can stand it—
For it is not an easy watch
It is not a relaxing narrative
It is not comfortable to feel for the character
The character who is you
Your forebear
Without whom you would not be here—
It is not easy to root for Kunta
To cheer for him
To hope 'the African' escapes.
Because you know that
For your great-granddaddy to find freedom
Is for you
To not be here
To vanish from this earth
To disappear from the typewriter pounding this
page.

You feel his pain
Taste his agony
You empathize with the masterful performance
Of a Louis Gossett, Jr.
The tear-jerking innocence and pride
Of a Levar Burton
Who plays the part you wanted.
But it goes much further than that
Your life is past

Decade-old resentment
For the part you swore was yours.

You wish you could call your uncle
And tell him how much you appreciate
Are affected by the tale, yet again
But he is gone.
He can revel in his words no more.
You can rejoice in his story
In your own history
Your uncle's offering to the world.
Still, ROOTS, is not an easy watch.
What will be your legacy?
How will you measure up
To Kunta

Kizzy
Chicken George
Matilda
Tom Murray
Irene
Will Palmer
Cynthia
Bertha, your grandmother
Simon, your grandfather
Julius, your father
Ida, your mother
George, your uncle
Alex, your uncle the world knows
Knew
What do you do
What do you do?

What do you do
To be you?
You don't know
But you're trying
Every day—
You're trying
And one day
You will find it
Your purpose
Your place in the family's memory
The world's memory.
Until then
It will be difficult
To watch ROOTS
Your beginning
One-fourth of your beginning
Which has made it so hard
To find
To carve
Your present.

The gift of Uncle Alex
The determination of Kinte
The residue of fame
With which you grapple
Yours to court
Yours to discern
Yours to earn.

Yes
Say your name Kunta Kinte
Say it at the slave driver's urging

By the whip
Toby.

Say your name, Chris
Have others say it
Because it is your name
Not because it evokes another's.

ROOTS is not an easy watch.
Root for the hero to escape
But make that hero you
And free the shadow
Of a line so proud and prominent.
Find your track
Be your own driver
Don't let your family
Stand in the way
But push on
Resolved
The Mandinka warrior remained
So you would know
This dilemma
Which you could
Which you would
Have no other way.

THE Mayor

Ever have a party?!

And nobody came?
Contemplate the reason
For your diminished fame?
Question when the luster left
Your once illustrious name?
Ever have a party and nobody came?

Ever say you're leaving and nobody give a
damn?
Find no one on the street
To hail your moving van.
Count the lack of "I'll miss you." pleas
To delay your exit plans.
Ever say you're leaving and nobody give a
damn?

Ever fear a nightmare
And waking find it true?
That no one had truly noticed
An insignificant you;
Tales of your popularity
Were overblown and misconstrued.
Ever fear a nightmare and waking find it true?

These things I've done and it hurts.
But there's nothing I can do

To change the way I lived
The last three years I knew.
I'll vanish in a week
To remember when I'm through
I left to just a whimper
Not the coveted ballyhoo.

And to think
I knew so many people
That they called me
The Mayor.

Christmas Suite

Part one

My Christmas Youth

Christmas eve
Thirty five of these
Which one was the best?
It's hard to say.
After 35
There are many lives
I've put to rest.

There was the infant me
What anticipation!
What anxiety!
The inability to sleep
Keen hearing detecting all whispers
Closed eyes seeing movement in the darkest
night
Waiting for the first peek of
Light through the window
No alarm
No school

But up like a shot
When Christmas was only presents
No family
No friends mattered as much as
The tunnel vision views of
Carefree minors
Who judged solely on
Santa's put out
Or not.

Part two

Conscientious Adolescence

Santa's teen years
When you've realized that
He's not
Sleep comes easier
Awakening comes later
To your peers you scoff
At the gifts you secretly desired alot
Neither are you as
Visibly disappointed
Over the items Santa forgot
First step toward maturity is
Masking unfulfilled feelings
Appreciating your parents for
What they tried
Accepting what you received
With a smile
Considering more what you have
Than have not.

Part three

Actor on Holiday

Christmas Holidays.
These peak days,
In theater,
Leave performers no ease.
One, two shows on the 25th;
The same on New Year's Eve.
I began to lose track
Of childhood awakenings and
Expecting some wonderful joy.
In the early 80's
All I was,
Was an energetic
"May I get you a cocktail, Ma'am?",
Pleased to serve you,
Acting boy.

Part four

Christmas Cheer/Domesticity

Then I had a life
A special existence
Interaction with another
A domestic relationship
I became two who joined and
Became one
And we had friends, a family.
A foundation of love,
Home and health;
Christmas rejuvenated!
We created a festival
An outrageous occasion
To drown our circle in gifts
We sat and opened all night
And found no space between us
When all was spread about
Christmas was a celebration
Of what we could do
For each other.
New Year's Eve completed the gaiety
The social highlight of the season
Happy to be within a loving community
Blessed to be with a beloved someone.

Afrocentric

ALI

Ali
I was shocked
I saw
I hadn't seen
I heard
I hadn't listened
Suddenly
I had to believe
I wanted to go away
I couldn't
As before I had been
Spellbound by his magic
I was now
Spellbound
By his vulnerability

In his honor I thought
Perhaps
I should cry
In his honor
I did not
As always
He commanded
Respect

He demanded
Admiration
Others who had
Reached his heights
Who could
"Float like a butterfly
And sting like a bee"
Would not have allowed
Their worshippers
Access to their
Humanity

How one who had been
Physically
So above us
Was now by disease
Impaired

The face
Still pretty
The wit
Twinkling in the eyes
Subdued movements
Strained speech
Saddened
Reminded
Excited

Imagine what combinations
He would dance
What lyrics
He would rhyme
If only his body
Would again obey his mind

The price for fame
Was a heavy one
Perhaps he soared too long
Immortality though
He has achieved
And knowing
It can never be
Taken from him
Transcends the faded skills

I could smile
I could leave.

Independence Day

The Fourth of July
I'm not sure, you see,
A day to celebrate
What historically was denied me.
No Blacks were freed
On that immortal date
No dark skinned souls leapt heights
House slaves served the parties
Field niggers watched the white folk
Dancing through the night
Both asked with silent stares
"How could massa think this is right?"
To salute the summer afternoon
Prance, drink, and be gay
Order more music, ice, fiddle playing,
Their bucks to caper songs;
Their females to accept evening visits,
Enjoying the people they blindly wrong.

Happy 4th of July
To America.
Happy Emancipation Declaration Day
January 1st 1863
To me.

LOVE

Remind me to forget you

Every night I remember to forget you,
But somehow the effort seems wrong.
There must be some good reason
You were sent in the first place.
To enjoy yourself.
And string me along.

I was your puppet.
You manipulated me.

But I welcomed the pull of your rope.
I cherished those moments, those nights,
When we'd hold each other.
My heart would tremble with hope.

Now,
I'm no longer wishful.
I've put those dreams aside.
Again
You've set me free with no warning
And only myself to deride.

In pain, I pray to heed my scorn,
Demand it burn a blister in my scalp

That will bubble, boil, and burst
  When I think of you...

  To remind me I'm glad I got out.

a song

Bake me cookies
Wink your eyes
Turn your back
And wave goodbye
Do whatever
I'll always be your friend.

Send me love songs
Black out my name
Write me poetry
And lay no claim
Do whatever
I'll always be your friend.

Phone me daily
Say its collect
Why you call
You always forget
Do whatever
I'll always be your friend.
Seems you want to set your hooks in me
Appears that I would like you to
But fear makes me wait to walk your way
If we become lovers
And then that ends
I've heard its impossible
To remain friends

Soooo...
Help me celebrate
My birthday date
Arrange the dinner
And arrive late
Do whatever
I'll always be your friend.

Declare you love me
You've shown you do
Protest the romance
That I owe you
Do whatever
I'll always be your friend.

Seems you want to set your hooks in me
Appears that I would like you to

But fear makes me wait to walk your way
If we become lovers
And then that ends
I've heard its impossible
To remain friends.

Bake me cookies
Wink your eyes
Turn your back
And wave goodbye
Do whatever
I'll
Do whatever
I'll

Do whatever
I'll always be your
But never more than your
Friend.

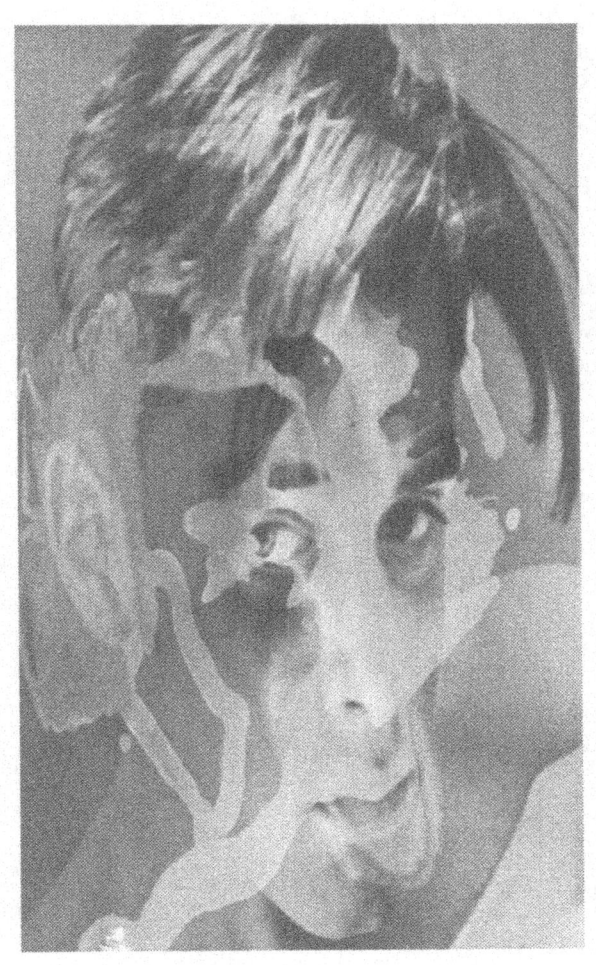

The same old ending

The end of 97
Another year in review
I've never relished recollections before
the summations rarely spill out new

Love attempted, love lost
Job endured, eternal cost
Independance gained
Dependency subdued
Relationships strengthened
Relationships screwed

97, January through December,
Another year and what have you come to?
A new address
And cash (more or less)
And that career
And that Love
Still that Love
Yet still
A heart beating to the same rhythm as yours
The eternal, neverending,
Unattained quest.

writing away

If writing took away misery
If it could eliminate thoughts of you
I'd scribble until my hands blistered
I'd bear down until my fingers turned blue

And I'd keep blistering and discoloring
My forearms numb
My elbows stiff and aching
Rigid from the incensed position
I'd forced them to maintain
My tense shoulders spasming
My swollen brain throbbing
My empty belly growling
Unfed for days
My butt burning
My legs cramping
From hours of not moving
And twitching at the same time

But if I was promised
My soul would feel
Lighter
After enduring this
That the tears I shed
Would be forgotten
For all time
Then I'd write until
My fingers broke in two
As badly mangled as my love was fractured
When I foolishly fell for you.

"writing away"   photo by john hopkins

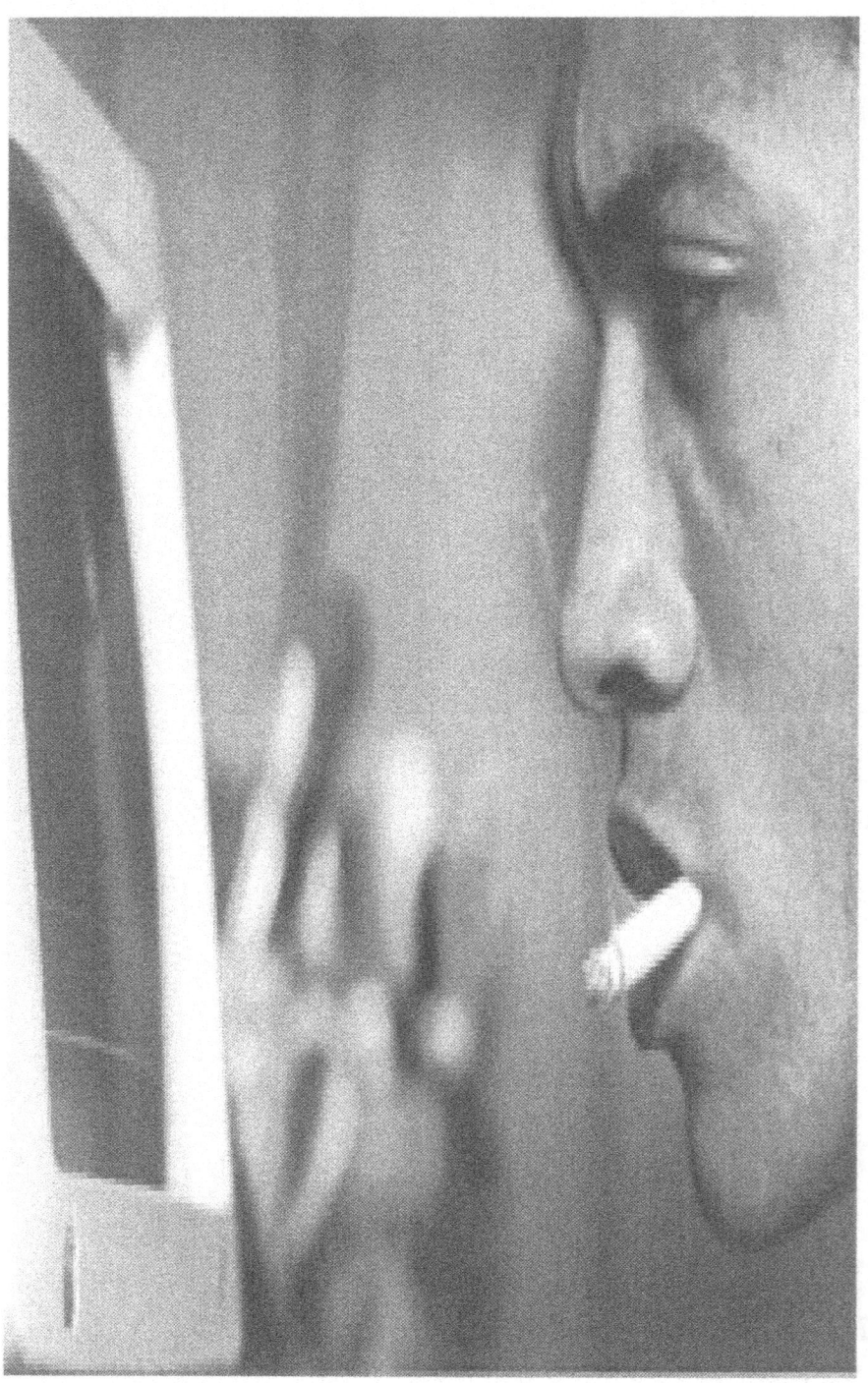

Career

the THEATRE and ME

Dove into a theater
To splash that part of me
From which talent flowed;
I didn't worry
I'd end up dry
I let the moment
Bear the load.
But the burden wasn't carried
My soul stayed asleep
My skills made no appearance
My eyes wouldn't weep
My emotions decided not to show.

Perhaps
I should have practiced
Should have rehearsed more
Than the verse.
Perhaps
I don't care anymore
Peut 'etre
Its even worse.

What happens when
You can't do
The only thing
You've wanted to?
When your glories
Seem fantasies
Indulged too long

44

Pushed too far
Until they became
A part of your being
You can't be
Anymore.

What do you do
When you can't do
What all your life
You thought
You were meant to do?
I'll never know
Until I'm dead
Then someone High
Will say to me
What down here
Was never said.
And I'll curse Him
For allowing me a lifetime
Of false hope.

The RACE

Ambition
Outruns drive
By a margin too large.

You know what you want
But are you scared to
To come get it?
I am out here,
Waiting,
Hands on my hips,
Tired of your delays.
I'm what you want
So what are you doing?

Afraid to dial a number,
Send a picture,

Speak my name
Success!

That's what they call me.
Many have been blessed
And not found happiness
I know
But will you ever be
Sure
Unless you do me?

No T.V.,
No Broadway,
No recording hits.
But can you sit there,
Lie there,
Take no classes,
Let auditions pass without a start,
And keep writing
This
Satisfied upon your death to just
Go?

If so
Let me know
Cause I've got better things to do
Than watch your ambition
Blown.

The purpose of critics

What is good?
Who tells you so
How do they decide
They really know

What have they done
To deserve the place
To decree what is worth saving
And what should be erased.

Aren't we all critics
Though we don't get paid as such
Judging our day to day lives
Rewriting when it hurts too much

At what point are we review proof
Secure from even our own self reproach
Likely never will we reach that nirvana
So its best to have other doubt slingers
Whose haughty words we can ridicule and roast.

King, Grisham, Rice, and me

Publishable
What makes it thus?
What makes some Stephen King
And others an embarrassing bust?

What make's one person's experiences
Riveting
While another's are biographical
Mush.
What deems one person's recollections
Pedestrian
While another's are lush?

I wish I knew these answers
I'd like to earn a buck or two
See my name
On the best sellers list
Be acclaimed
On the New York Times Book Review.

Fate's decreed I wait a little
Longer
Make sure fame doesn't overcome
My gross
Appreciation of what I've accomplished
Humoring my overworn house guest, 'patience'
Me, her well-established,
Overqualified, host.

Memo

Memo
Memorabilia
All things good and fine
A tattered pad helps you remember
The beautiful things you once did find
The pen is among those memories
Of when you were thirsty to write
To cram a page thick with illusions
You might act out one night
Give me that folder stuffed with yellowed papers
That box jammed with scratched floppy discs
That have grown so dated next to
21st century tools for visual inscription
And storing records electronically, invisible to sight.
In any form
These writings remain vital
That they matter still is right
Letters and reminders of
Sad and gay times
Of friends many lifetimes away
As weightless now in your bittersweet memory
As the tissue
Which wipes that tear each day

Memo
Memorabilia
Items you protect and save

Did they mean more to you then
Or has meaning grown awaiting your grave
Will a string represent some
Last thought
When those last moments race by
Or will time be deemed immeasurable
When nothing else materializes to
Close
Your
Eyes

Scold me
If I get too maudlin
Chide me
If I get too shy
Why waste time waxing poetic
If all I spin
Is a lie

Memo
Memorabilia
This, too,
Will be one of those
Copied, printed, and stored away
Self analyzed until it is cold.
Was it good
Was it real
Was it
Special
Did it make you relate
Did you feel
Did it matter at all that

I wrote this?
Who cares
So what
Its written
Cut the artistic doubt
Deal.

*On the Sadly Outdated State of Affairs
Which Was...*

The O.J. Suite

WEDDING

In the light of divorce,
Pain and recrimination,
In the glare of domestic violence,
Brutality and death,
Dwarfed by the shadow of all this,
Allow me to spin
A perfect tale.

The blending of spirits and
The mixing of blood,
The celebration and declaration of love;
A wedding.
Could it last
As sweet as begun?
"For worse" would never happen
And life end beautifully sung
That special day
The moment when
Husband and Wife are one.

The new couple kiss
And affectionately hug.
They face their audience
And raise their hands high.
Radiating joy and triumph,
Completion,
They beam
Happy as they have ever been,

Warmer than they have ever felt,
More secure than they ever imagined possible.

The crowd cheers.
Mothers cry.
Fathers shake hands and wipe
Their moistened eyes.
Then
All stare silently
As the couple embraces again,
Tighter this time;
Their grips leave impressions.
The small child,
Which they agreed to produce
Before they wed,
Is led to them
By the minister
Who helps the boy,
Innocent of his role,
Raise the cup
To his parents'
Determined lips.
Sipping of the contents
They kneel and kiss their heir.

The Mothers moan.
The Fathers sob.
The couple assures all
"We're the happiest we can ever be."

Their legs buckle.
The minister directs the ushers,

As rehearsed,
To hold the newlyweds
And lower them
Onto the queen size bed of feathers,
Mounted on the slanted raised platform,
So all can see
Their heads touch the pillows,
Their gazes connect,
The tear that washes her cheek,
The two which dampen his.
They kiss once more,
Long and tender,
Lay back,
Close their eyes
And smile.
They lived to achieve the
Ultimate moment
And having found it chose
Their life should be done.

This was the perfect tale of
Two people
Who knew only happiness and
Refused to know
Anything else
And anything more.

GLUT

Nine books on the shelf
More throughout the stacks
Carrying different titles
Various slanted views
I wondered why the shelf
Didn't have its own sign
Like the other literary genres
Fiction, Non-Fiction, Romance, Mystery- O.J.
Of course.
It wasn't necessary.

Do you remember where you were
When you first heard the news
And it was just
A passing story?
Do you recall
When the story was small?
I was driving home from work
It was sunny
It was June
Something about O.J.'s ex-wife, murdered.

The T.V. screen showed him
In handcuffs
I thought "How awful.
They wouldn't have done that
To a white guy.
Take 'em off."

And they did.
He was in Chicago after all
Oh, he was in L.A. when it happened.
The story had grown tall.

Our parents remember J.F.K.
And where they were
That fatal day
I was home from work
By my set I stayed
I watched the Ford Bronco crawl away
How surreal it was
Will we see his head explode
The Zapruder tape had nothing on this
World wide coverage on an open road

But where were you when the verdict was read
The first verdict
The President spoke over the second
I was in a mixed crowd
"We find the defendant...Not Guilty."
A White woman said
"He got away with it."

A Black man said
"He ought to sue everybody!"
Black me who thought he did it
Said nothing.

So what do you think of
Knit caps now?
Gloves?

Golf Clubs?
Lawyers?
Police?
Judges?
Media?
Bruno Magli, "...those ugly ass shoes."

Can we revisit the sports hero
And the common man?
O.J. is one for two
Joe Blow would have gone zero
The richness of his class
saved him
The vengeance of his class
brought him back
To the people he appealed to-
The Black poor.

Book after book after book
On one man
By authors, acquaintances, detectives,
Lawyers, girlfriends, jurors, and more
Digging a hole
We all sank into
Wallowing in a glut of misery
A pool of pain and blood
Thankful it wasn't ours
But too engrossed to let it go.
Let go, America
Let go.

Lizzie and O.J.

Slash, slash
Make a dash
Run away
And very fast.
Fly to Chicago,
Elude L.A.,
Confident you'll score
You are O.J.

Years pass
People dead, still two.
You emerge undefeated
Criminal trial through

Civil jury impaneled
Judge a harsher foe
Since Rodney got his the second time
Your doom's spelled
Quid Pro Quo

Pockets now empty
Cupboard past bare
Your children in limbo
Public doesn't care

They enjoyed the titillation
Of a tragedy rerun
With no answer
But two solutions
For a murder yet undone

60

If it was you
You should have slashed yourself
If not
You shouldn't have run
Like Lizzie Borden
Your fate is sealed
Number 32
The infamous one.

COWARD

"He won't kill himself;"
Said the ex-wife of another
Superstar athlete
Who had suffered
Almost the same
As her fallen friend
"Any man who beats on his wife
Is a coward.
He's too much of a coward
To commit suicide."

I had heard this before
To kill oneself is
Cowardly.
"A coward's way out."
In war
The soldier runs
Afraid to die
In peace
The rocker shoots himself
Afraid to live.

Some in the athlete's
Army of crushed fans
Wished he had ended the chase
The respectful procession to his home
Decisively
With finality
To spare us

The deflating days, nights,
And months
Which will leave us years
Of memories
Of our shameful interest
Our insatiable appetite
At the despair of another.
Thoughts to gnaw at our souls
Our pride
The fear within us
That we
Each disbelieving one
Could do the same
Unthinkable act.

I would rather be a coward
Than face that.

O.J. Country

Well
It's over
Said and Done
And once again he's
On the run
From what he did
Or didn't do
And what we think
Me and you
He is free
And on his own
Left offenders
Better known
And his defenders
Higher paid
And his future
Sadly paved
With the memory
Of two lost souls
Left unavenged
Left unwhole
Their spirits circling
The Brentwood Estate
Replaying a nightmare
They couldn't escape
If he did it
We'll never know
And if it was others
It will only show

A nation divided
Over class and race
May lay unrivaled claim
To a tarnished face.

Brief Thoughts

questions

Do I need what I want
When I want it?

Do I get what I need
When I should?

Do I achieve what I desire
because I deserve it?

Are the questions I ask
Any good?

Weather Report

People always talk
About saving
For a rainy day.
I don't want
To go out when its raining.
Give me some money
When the sun's out.

MOVE ON

You do
What you do
When you do it;
When you do it
It's through.
Get over it
Get past it
It's done.

The Olympics

The Olympics can be
So golden
The victories ever so
Sweet
The defeats
Terribly monstrous
The quest incomparably
Complete.

And
1 4
the Road

As my life moves on

As my life moves on
And my past fades
I wonder and remember
What I did from day to day.

If something had occurred
Differently
Which other worlds
Might I have explored
Or was everything decided
When my mother screamed me forth?

Can anyone ever
Change their life?
If you swear you have
Do you really know
That what you chose
You truly chose
You weren't ordered to
By the One who knows.

Enjoy the ride
Drift on the flow
Marvel at the tides
Which softly roll
Hold on as the track
Dips you upside down
And sets you aright
Smiling that you've found
Peace.